THIS JOURNAL BELONGS TO

IF FOUND, PLEASE CALL

ONWE PRESENTS

doing

FROM DREAMS TO REALITY

ONWE

ONWE

For more daily motivation and prompts
follow us on Instagram @weareonwe

For more books,
questions or suggestions: www.onwe.co

First published in Great Britain in 2021 by Onwe Press Ltd

This hardback edition was first published in 2021

Printed and bounded by Clays Printers (UK) Ltd,
Elcograf S.p.A.

Cover Design by Mariam Jimoh

A CIP catalogue record for this book is available from the British
Library.

Hardback ISBN 978-1-913872-08-3

"WHATEVER YOU CAN
DO OR DREAM YOU
CAN, BEGIN IT;
BOLDNESS HAS
GENIUS, POWER, AND
MAGIC IN IT"

Johann Wolfgang von Goethe

CONTENT

Page 9   **Introduction**

Page 9   Journaling your dreams into a reality

Page 11   **Tracking and Reflections**

Page 11   Month 1
Page 14   Week 1
Page 30   Week 2
Page 46   Week 3
Page 62   Week 4
Page 77   Bonus days

Page 85   Month 2
Page 91   Week 1
Page 106   Week 2
Page 122   Week 3
Page 138   Week 4
Page 153   Bonus days

Page 161   Month 3
Page 166   Week 1
Page 182   Week 2
Page 198   Week 3
Page 214   Week 4
Page 229   Bonus days

Page 238   **Common Dreams**

Page 243   **Notes & Ideas**

Page 256   **References**

an introduction.

JOURNALING YOUR DREAM INTO A REALITY

Over 7 billion people across the planet share one common thing: we dream. There are some we can't remember, some take over our waking days, and a few special dreams become reality.

The people who often seem to make their waking dreams come true don't have access to a magic lamp, a jinn lurking in the shadows, or even to a fairy godmother. These successful people simply follow the essential steps—one at a time—to reach their goals.

The Art of Doing is certainly not as easy as it sounds though. That's why so many people around the world struggle to move consistently towards their goals. Our dreams can seem so lofty and far removed from our current situation—and the journey towards them can appear almost impossible—so that even the first step is dogged by fears and anxieties. These are real emotions that can seriously hold us back from realising our dreams and desires.

Thankfully, we've found a way round the obstacles. Behavioural scientists have found that prompting people to make plans significantly increases the chances of follow-through. In other words, good planning can help you to do.

This journal is designed to assist you on the path to reaching your goals and dreams. You'll find daily, weekly and monthly planning prompts for the next 12-weeks to spur you on. The behaviour trackers and reflections included will also go a long way in facilitating your transformation into the ultimate do-er.

month one.

TAKE A DEEP BREATH

	MON	TUE	WED	THU

IDEAS

FRI	SAT	SUN	
			NOTES

REFLECTIONS

DATE _____

MY INTENTION FOR THE DAY IS

_____

_____

THIS IS HOW I WILL MAKE TODAY GREAT

_____

_____

TOP THREE TASKS

- ○ _____
- ○ _____
- ○ _____

OTHER TASKS

- ○ _____
- ○ _____
- ○ _____
- ○ _____
- ○ _____
- ○ _____
- ○ _____
- ○ _____
- ○ _____
- ○ _____
- ○ _____
- ○ _____
- ○ _____

DAILY SCHEDULE

TIME	TASK

DAILY TRACKER

LAST NIGHT, I DREAMT

___

___

___

MY BEST THOUGHTS WERE

___

___

___

MY REWARD FOR MEETING MY GOALS IS

___

___

___

TODAY, I FEEL

EXCELLENT   GOOD   REGULAR   SAD   ANGRY

DAILY TRACKER

SLEEP

DATE _____

MY INTENTION FOR THE DAY IS

_____

_____

THIS IS HOW I WILL MAKE TODAY GREAT

_____

_____

TOP THREE TASKS

- ○ _____
- ○ _____
- ○ _____

OTHER TASKS

- ○ _____
- ○ _____
- ○ _____
- ○ _____
- ○ _____
- ○ _____
- ○ _____
- ○ _____
- ○ _____
- ○ _____
- ○ _____
- ○ _____
- ○ _____

DAILY SCHEDULE

TIME	TASK

DAILY TRACKER

LAST NIGHT, I DREAMT

_____

_____

_____

MY BEST THOUGHTS WERE

_____

_____

_____

MY REWARD FOR MEETING MY GOALS IS

_____

_____

_____

TODAY, I FEEL

EXCELLENT   GOOD   REGULAR   SAD   ANGRY

DAILY TRACKER

SLEEP

DATE _____   (M T W T F S S

MY INTENTION FOR THE DAY IS

_____

_____

THIS IS HOW I WILL MAKE TODAY GREAT

_____

TOP THREE TASKS

- ○ _____
- ○ _____
- ○ _____

OTHER TASKS

- ○ _____
- ○ _____
- ○ _____
- ○ _____
- ○ _____
- ○ _____
- ○ _____
- ○ _____
- ○ _____
- ○ _____
- ○ _____
- ○ _____
- ○ _____

DAILY SCHEDULE

TIME	TASK

DAILY TRACKER

LAST NIGHT, I DREAMT

MY BEST THOUGHTS WERE

MY REWARD FOR MEETING MY GOALS IS

TODAY, I FEEL

EXCELLENT   GOOD   REGULAR   SAD   ANGRY

DAILY TRACKER

SLEEP

19

DATE _____

MY INTENTION FOR THE DAY IS

_____

_____

THIS IS HOW I WILL MAKE TODAY GREAT

_____

_____

TOP THREE TASKS

- ○ _____
- ○ _____
- ○ _____

OTHER TASKS

- ○ _____
- ○ _____
- ○ _____
- ○ _____
- ○ _____
- ○ _____
- ○ _____
- ○ _____
- ○ _____
- ○ _____
- ○ _____
- ○ _____
- ○ _____

DAILY SCHEDULE

TIME	TASK

DAILY TRACKER

LAST NIGHT, I DREAMT

MY BEST THOUGHTS WERE

MY REWARD FOR MEETING MY GOALS IS

TODAY, I FEEL

EXCELLENT   GOOD   REGULAR   SAD   ANGRY

DAILY TRACKER

WATER

SLEEP

DATE _____

MY INTENTION FOR THE DAY IS

_____

_____

THIS IS HOW I WILL MAKE TODAY GREAT

_____

TOP THREE TASKS

- ○ _____
- ○ _____
- ○ _____

OTHER TASKS

- ○ _____
- ○ _____
- ○ _____
- ○ _____
- ○ _____
- ○ _____
- ○ _____
- ○ _____
- ○ _____
- ○ _____
- ○ _____
- ○ _____

DAILY SCHEDULE

TIME	TASK

DAILY TRACKER

LAST NIGHT, I DREAMT

MY BEST THOUGHTS WERE

MY REWARD FOR MEETING MY GOALS IS

TODAY, I FEEL

EXCELLENT

GOOD

REGULAR

SAD

ANGRY

DAILY TRACKER

WATER

SLEEP

DATE _____   M T W T F S S

MY INTENTION FOR THE DAY IS

_____

_____

THIS IS HOW I WILL MAKE TODAY GREAT

_____

_____

TOP THREE TASKS

○ _____

○ _____

○ _____

OTHER TASKS

○ _____
○ _____
○ _____
○ _____
○ _____
○ _____
○ _____
○ _____
○ _____
○ _____
○ _____
○ _____
○ _____

DAILY SCHEDULE

TIME	TASK

DAILY TRACKER

LAST NIGHT, I DREAMT

_____

_____

_____

MY BEST THOUGHTS WERE

_____

_____

_____

MY REWARD FOR MEETING MY GOALS IS

_____

_____

_____

TODAY, I FEEL

| EXCELLENT | GOOD | REGULAR | SAD | ANGRY |

DAILY TRACKER

WATER

SLEEP

DATE _____

MY INTENTION FOR THE DAY IS

_____

_____

THIS IS HOW I WILL MAKE TODAY GREAT

_____

_____

TOP THREE TASKS

- ○ _____
- ○ _____
- ○ _____

OTHER TASKS

- ○ _____
- ○ _____
- ○ _____
- ○ _____
- ○ _____
- ○ _____
- ○ _____
- ○ _____
- ○ _____
- ○ _____
- ○ _____
- ○ _____
- ○ _____

DAILY SCHEDULE

TIME	TASK

DAILY TRACKER

LAST NIGHT, I DREAMT

MY BEST THOUGHTS WERE

MY REWARD FOR MEETING MY GOALS IS

TODAY, I FEEL

EXCELLENT

GOOD

REGULAR

SAD

ANGRY

DAILY TRACKER

SLEEP

TO ACCOMPLISH GREAT THINGS WE MUST NOT ONLY ACT, BUT ALSO DREAM; NOT ONLY PLAN, BUT ALSO BELIEVE.

Anatole France

WEEKLY TRACKER

MY WEEKLY WINS

THIS WEEK, I LEARNT

HABIT TRACKER

HABIT	M	T	W	T	F	S	S
	●	●	●	●	●	●	●
	●	●	●	●	●	●	●
	●	●	●	●	●	●	●

MY TASKS FOR NEXT WEEK

○

○

○

○

○

○

○

DATE _____

MY INTENTION FOR THE DAY IS

_____

_____

THIS IS HOW I WILL MAKE TODAY GREAT

_____

TOP THREE TASKS

- ○ _____
- ○ _____
- ○ _____

OTHER TASKS

- ○ _____
- ○ _____
- ○ _____
- ○ _____
- ○ _____
- ○ _____
- ○ _____
- ○ _____
- ○ _____
- ○ _____
- ○ _____
- ○ _____
- ○ _____

DAILY SCHEDULE

TIME	TASK

DAILY TRACKER

LAST NIGHT, I DREAMT

MY BEST THOUGHTS WERE

MY REWARD FOR MEETING MY GOALS IS

TODAY, I FEEL

EXCELLENT   GOOD   REGULAR   SAD   ANGRY

DAILY TRACKER

SLEEP

DATE _____   (M T W T F S S

MY INTENTION FOR THE DAY IS

_____

_____

THIS IS HOW I WILL MAKE TODAY GREAT

_____

TOP THREE TASKS

O _____

O _____

O _____

OTHER TASKS

O _____

O _____

O _____

O _____

O _____

O _____

O _____

O _____

O _____

O _____

O _____

O _____

O _____

DAILY SCHEDULE

TIME	TASK

DAILY TRACKER

LAST NIGHT, I DREAMT

MY BEST THOUGHTS WERE

MY REWARD FOR MEETING MY GOALS IS

TODAY, I FEEL

EXCELLENT   GOOD   REGULAR   SAD   ANGRY

DAILY TRACKER

  SLEEP

DATE _____

MY INTENTION FOR THE DAY IS

_____

_____

THIS IS HOW I WILL MAKE TODAY GREAT

_____

_____

TOP THREE TASKS

O _____

O _____

O _____

OTHER TASKS

O _____

O _____

O _____

O _____

O _____

O _____

O _____

O _____

O _____

O _____

O _____

O _____

O _____

DAILY SCHEDULE

TIME	TASK

DAILY TRACKER

LAST NIGHT, I DREAMT

MY BEST THOUGHTS WERE

MY REWARD FOR MEETING MY GOALS IS

TODAY, I FEEL

EXCELLENT   GOOD   REGULAR   SAD   ANGRY

DAILY TRACKER

SLEEP

DATE _____

MY INTENTION FOR THE DAY IS

_____

_____

THIS IS HOW I WILL MAKE TODAY GREAT

_____

TOP THREE TASKS

○ _____
○ _____
○ _____

OTHER TASKS

○ _____
○ _____
○ _____
○ _____
○ _____
○ _____
○ _____
○ _____
○ _____
○ _____
○ _____
○ _____
○ _____

DAILY SCHEDULE

TIME	TASK

DAILY TRACKER

LAST NIGHT, I DREAMT

MY BEST THOUGHTS WERE

MY REWARD FOR MEETING MY GOALS IS

TODAY, I FEEL

EXCELLENT	GOOD	REGULAR	SAD	ANGRY

DAILY TRACKER

WATER

SLEEP

DATE _____ M T W T F S S

MY INTENTION FOR THE DAY IS

_____

_____

THIS IS HOW I WILL MAKE TODAY GREAT

_____

TOP THREE TASKS

- ○ _____
- ○ _____
- ○ _____

OTHER TASKS

- ○ _____
- ○ _____
- ○ _____
- ○ _____
- ○ _____
- ○ _____
- ○ _____
- ○ _____
- ○ _____
- ○ _____
- ○ _____
- ○ _____
- ○ _____

DAILY SCHEDULE

TIME	TASK

DAILY TRACKER

LAST NIGHT, I DREAMT

MY BEST THOUGHTS WERE

MY REWARD FOR MEETING MY GOALS IS

TODEY, I FEEL

EXCELLENT   GOOD   REGULAR   SAD   ANGRY

DAILY TRACKER

WATER   SLEEP

DATE _____

MY INTENTION FOR THE DAY IS

_____

_____

THIS IS HOW I WILL MAKE TODAY GREAT

_____

TOP THREE TASKS

- ○ _____
- ○ _____
- ○ _____

OTHER TASKS

- ○ _____
- ○ _____
- ○ _____
- ○ _____
- ○ _____
- ○ _____
- ○ _____
- ○ _____
- ○ _____
- ○ _____
- ○ _____
- ○ _____
- ○ _____

DAILY SCHEDULE

TIME	TASK

DAILY TRACKER

LAST NIGHT, I DREAMT

MY BEST THOUGHTS WERE

MY REWARD FOR MEETING MY GOALS IS

TODAY, I FEEL

| EXCELLENT | GOOD | REGULAR | SAD | ANGRY |

DAILY TRACKER

WATER

SLEEP

DATE _____   (M T W T F S S

MY INTENTION FOR THE DAY IS

_____

_____

THIS IS HOW I WILL MAKE TODAY GREAT

_____

_____

TOP THREE TASKS

- ○ _____
- ○ _____
- ○ _____

OTHER TASKS

- ○ _____
- ○ _____
- ○ _____
- ○ _____
- ○ _____
- ○ _____
- ○ _____
- ○ _____
- ○ _____
- ○ _____
- ○ _____
- ○ _____
- ○ _____

DAILY SCHEDULE

TIME	TASK

DAILY TRACKER

LAST NIGHT, I DREAMT

_____

_____

_____

MY BEST THOUGHTS WERE

_____

_____

MY REWARD FOR MEETING MY GOALS IS

_____

_____

_____

TODAY, I FEEL

EXCELLENT

GOOD

REGULAR

SAD

ANGRY

DAILY TRACKER

SLEEP

DREAMS DO NOT
COME TRUE JUST
BECAUSE YOU DREAM
THEM. IT'S HARD
WORK THAT MAKES
THINGS HAPPEN.IT'S
HARD WORK THAT
CREATES CHANGE.

Shonda Rhimes

WEEKLY TRACKER

MY WEEKLY WINS

THIS WEEK, I LEARNT

HABIT TRACKER

HABIT	M	T	W	T	F	S	S
	●	●	●	●	●	●	●
	●	●	●	●	●	●	●
	●	●	●	●	●	●	●

MY TASKS FOR NEXT WEEK

- ○
- ○
- ○
- ○
- ○
- ○
- ○

DATE _____

MY INTENTION FOR THE DAY IS

_____

_____

THIS IS HOW I WILL MAKE TODAY GREAT

_____

_____

TOP THREE TASKS

○ _____

○ _____

○ _____

OTHER TASKS

○ _____
○ _____
○ _____
○ _____
○ _____
○ _____
○ _____
○ _____
○ _____
○ _____
○ _____
○ _____
○ _____

DAILY SCHEDULE

TIME	TASK

DAILY TRACKER

LAST NIGHT, I DREAMT

_____

_____

_____

MY BEST THOUGHTS WERE

_____

_____

_____

MY REWARD FOR MEETING MY GOALS IS

_____

_____

_____

TODAY, I FEEL

EXCELLENT

GOOD

REGULAR

SAD

ANGRY

DAILY TRACKER

 SLEEP

47

DATE _____   (M T W T F S S

MY INTENTION FOR THE DAY IS

_____

_____

THIS IS HOW I WILL MAKE TODAY GREAT

_____

TOP THREE TASKS

○ _____

○ _____

○ _____

OTHER TASKS

○ _____

○ _____

○ _____

○ _____

○ _____

○ _____

○ _____

○ _____

○ _____

○ _____

○ _____

○ _____

○ _____

DAILY SCHEDULE

TIME	TASK

DAILY TRACKER

LAST NIGHT, I DREAMT

MY BEST THOUGHTS WERE

MY REWARD FOR MEETING MY GOALS IS

TODAY, I FEEL

EXCELLENT   GOOD   REGULAR   SAD   ANGRY

DAILY TRACKER

SLEEP

DATE _____

MY INTENTION FOR THE DAY IS

_____

_____

THIS IS HOW I WILL MAKE TODAY GREAT

_____

_____

TOP THREE TASKS

- ◯ _____
- ◯ _____
- ◯ _____

OTHER TASKS

- ◯ _____
- ◯ _____
- ◯ _____
- ◯ _____
- ◯ _____
- ◯ _____
- ◯ _____
- ◯ _____
- ◯ _____
- ◯ _____
- ◯ _____
- ◯ _____
- ◯ _____

DAILY SCHEDULE

TIME	TASK

DAILY TRACKER

LAST NIGHT, I DREAMT

MY BEST THOUGHTS WERE

MY REWARD FOR MEETING MY GOALS IS

TODAY, I FEEL

EXCELLENT	GOOD	REGULAR	SAD	ANGRY

DAILY TRACKER

SLEEP

DATE _____   (M T W T F S S

MY INTENTION FOR THE DAY IS

_____

_____

THIS IS HOW I WILL MAKE TODAY GREAT

_____

_____

TOP THREE TASKS

○ _____
○ _____
○ _____

OTHER TASKS

○ _____
○ _____
○ _____
○ _____
○ _____
○ _____
○ _____
○ _____
○ _____
○ _____
○ _____
○ _____
○ _____

DAILY SCHEDULE

TIME	TASK

DAILY TRACKER

LAST NIGHT, I DREAMT

MY BEST THOUGHTS WERE

MY REWARD FOR MEETING MY GOALS IS

TODAY, I FEEL

EXCELLENT   GOOD   REGULAR   SAD   ANGRY

DAILY TRACKER

WATER

SLEEP

DATE _____

MY INTENTION FOR THE DAY IS

_____

_____

THIS IS HOW I WILL MAKE TODAY GREAT

_____

_____

TOP THREE TASKS

- ○ _____
- ○ _____
- ○ _____

OTHER TASKS

- ○ _____
- ○ _____
- ○ _____
- ○ _____
- ○ _____
- ○ _____
- ○ _____
- ○ _____
- ○ _____
- ○ _____
- ○ _____
- ○ _____
- ○ _____

DAILY SCHEDULE

TIME	TASK

DAILY TRACKER

LAST NIGHT, I DREAMT

_____

_____

_____

MY BEST THOUGHTS WERE

_____

_____

_____

MY REWARD FOR MEETING MY GOALS IS

_____

_____

_____

TODAY, I FEEL

EXCELLENT

GOOD

REGULAR

SAD

ANGRY

DAILY TRACKER

WATER

SLEEP

DATE _____

MY INTENTION FOR THE DAY IS

_____

_____

THIS IS HOW I WILL MAKE TODAY GREAT

_____

TOP THREE TASKS

- ○ _____
- ○ _____
- ○ _____

OTHER TASKS

- ○ _____
- ○ _____
- ○ _____
- ○ _____
- ○ _____
- ○ _____
- ○ _____
- ○ _____
- ○ _____
- ○ _____
- ○ _____
- ○ _____
- ○ _____

DAILY SCHEDULE

TIME	TASK

DAILY TRACKER

LAST NIGHT, I DREAMT

MY BEST THOUGHTS WERE

MY REWARD FOR MEETING MY GOALS IS

TODAY, I FEEL

EXCELLENT   GOOD   REGULAR   SAD   ANGRY

DAILY TRACKER

SLEEP

DATE _____   M T W T F S S

MY INTENTION FOR THE DAY IS

_____

_____

THIS IS HOW I WILL MAKE TODAY GREAT

_____

TOP THREE TASKS

- ○ _____
- ○ _____
- ○ _____

OTHER TASKS

- ○ _____
- ○ _____
- ○ _____
- ○ _____
- ○ _____
- ○ _____
- ○ _____
- ○ _____
- ○ _____
- ○ _____
- ○ _____
- ○ _____
- ○ _____

DAILY SCHEDULE

TIME	TASK

DAILY TRACKER

LAST NIGHT, I DREAMT

MY BEST THOUGHTS WERE

MY REWARD FOR MEETING MY GOALS IS

TODAY, I FEEL

EXCELLENT   GOOD   REGULAR   SAD   ANGRY

DAILY TRACKER

SLEEP

THE MOST EFFECTIVE WAY TO DO IT IS TO DO IT.

Amelia Earhart

WEEKLY TRACKER

MY WEEKLY WINS

THIS WEEK, I LEARNT

HABIT TRACKER

HABIT	M	T	W	T	F	S	S

MY TASKS FOR NEXT WEEK

○
○
○
○
○
○
○

DATE _____   (M T W T F S S

MY INTENTION FOR THE DAY IS

_____

_____

THIS IS HOW I WILL MAKE TODAY GREAT

_____

_____

TOP THREE TASKS

O _____
O _____
O _____

OTHER TASKS

O _____
O _____
O _____
O _____
O _____
O _____
O _____
O _____
O _____
O _____
O _____
O _____
O _____

DAILY SCHEDULE

TIME	TASK

DAILY TRACKER

LAST NIGHT, I DREAMT

_____

_____

_____

MY BEST THOUGHTS WERE

_____

_____

_____

MY REWARD FOR MEETING MY GOALS IS

_____

_____

_____

TODAY, I FEEL

EXCELLENT   GOOD   REGULAR   SAD   ANGRY

DAILY TRACKER

SLEEP

DATE _____   (M T W T F S S)

_____

_____

THIS IS HOW I WILL MAKE TODAY GREAT

_____

_____

TOP THREE TASKS

- O _____
- O _____
- O _____

OTHER TASKS

- O _____
- O _____
- O _____
- O _____
- O _____
- O _____
- O _____
- O _____
- O _____
- O _____
- O _____
- O _____
- O _____

DAILY SCHEDULE

TIME	TASK

DAILY TRACKER

LAST NIGHT, I DREAMT

MY BEST THOUGHTS WERE

MY REWARD FOR MEETING MY GOALS IS

TODAY, I FEEL

EXCELLENT

GOOD

REGULAR

SAD

ANGRY

DAILY TRACKER

SLEEP

DATE _____   (M T W T F S S

_____

_____

THIS IS HOW I WILL MAKE TODAY GREAT

_____

_____

TOP THREE TASKS

- ○ _____
- ○ _____
- ○ _____

OTHER TASKS

- ○ _____
- ○ _____
- ○ _____
- ○ _____
- ○ _____
- ○ _____
- ○ _____
- ○ _____
- ○ _____
- ○ _____
- ○ _____
- ○ _____
- ○ _____

DAILY SCHEDULE

TIME	TASK

DAILY TRACKER

LAST NIGHT, I DREAMT

MY BEST THOUGHTS WERE

MY REWARD FOR MEETING MY GOALS IS

TODAY, I FEEL

EXCELLENT　　GOOD　　REGULAR　　SAD　　ANGRY

DAILY TRACKER

SLEEP

DATE _____

MY INTENTION FOR THE DAY IS

_____

_____

THIS IS HOW I WILL MAKE TODAY GREAT

_____

_____

TOP THREE TASKS

O _____

O _____

O _____

OTHER TASKS

O _____
O _____
O _____
O _____
O _____
O _____
O _____
O _____
O _____
O _____
O _____
O _____
O _____

DAILY SCHEDULE

TIME	TASK

DAILY TRACKER

LAST NIGHT, I DREAMT

MY BEST THOUGHTS WERE

MY REWARD FOR MEETING MY GOALS IS

TODAY, I FEEL

| EXCELLENT | GOOD | REGULAR | SAD | ANGRY |

DAILY TRACKER

DATE _____

MY INTENTION FOR THE DAY IS

_____

_____

THIS IS HOW I WILL MAKE TODAY GREAT

_____

_____

TOP THREE TASKS

- O _____
- O _____
- O _____

OTHER TASKS

- O _____
- O _____
- O _____
- O _____
- O _____
- O _____
- O _____
- O _____
- O _____
- O _____
- O _____
- O _____
- O _____

DAILY SCHEDULE

TIME	TASK

DAILY TRACKER

LAST NIGHT, I DREAMT

MY BEST THOUGHTS WERE

MY REWARD FOR MEETING MY GOALS IS

TODAY, I FEEL

EXCELLENT   GOOD   REGULAR   SAD   ANGRY

DAILY TRACKER

WATER   SLEEP

DATE _____   (M T W T F S S)

MY INTENTION FOR THE DAY IS

_____

_____

THIS IS HOW I WILL MAKE TODAY GREAT

_____

TOP THREE TASKS

- ○ _____
- ○ _____
- ○ _____

OTHER TASKS

- ○ _____
- ○ _____
- ○ _____
- ○ _____
- ○ _____
- ○ _____
- ○ _____
- ○ _____
- ○ _____
- ○ _____
- ○ _____
- ○ _____
- ○ _____

DAILY SCHEDULE

TIME	TASK

DAILY TRACKER

LAST NIGHT, I DREAMT

MY BEST THOUGHTS WERE

MY REWARD FOR MEETING MY GOALS IS

TODAY, I FEEL

EXCELLENT   GOOD   REGULAR   SAD   ANGRY

DAILY TRACKER

SLEEP

DATE _____   (M T W T F S S

MY INTENTION FOR THE DAY IS

_____

_____

THIS IS HOW I WILL MAKE TODAY GREAT

_____

TOP THREE TASKS

- ◯ _____
- ◯ _____
- ◯ _____

OTHER TASKS

- ◯ _____
- ◯ _____
- ◯ _____
- ◯ _____
- ◯ _____
- ◯ _____
- ◯ _____
- ◯ _____
- ◯ _____
- ◯ _____
- ◯ _____
- ◯ _____
- ◯ _____

DAILY SCHEDULE

TIME	TASK

DAILY TRACKER

LAST NIGHT, I DREAMT

MY BEST THOUGHTS WERE

MY REWARD FOR MEETING MY GOALS IS

TODAY, I FEEL

EXCELLENT

GOOD

REGULAR

SAD

ANGRY

DAILY TRACKER

SLEEP

IT'S NOT WHAT WE DO
ONCE IN A WHILE THAT
SHAPES OUR LIVES,
BUT WHAT WE DO
CONSISTENTLY.

Tony Robbins

bonus days.

TAKE CARE

DATE _____   (M T W T F S S

MY INTENTION FOR THE DAY IS

_____

_____

THIS IS HOW I WILL MAKE TODAY GREAT

_____

TOP THREE TASKS

- ○ _____
- ○ _____
- ○ _____

OTHER TASKS

- ○ _____
- ○ _____
- ○ _____
- ○ _____
- ○ _____
- ○ _____
- ○ _____
- ○ _____
- ○ _____
- ○ _____
- ○ _____
- ○ _____
- ○ _____

DAILY SCHEDULE

TIME	TASK

DAILY TRACKER

LAST NIGHT, I DREAMT

MY BEST THOUGHTS WERE

MY REWARD FOR MEETING MY GOALS IS

TODAY, I FEEL

EXCELLENT

GOOD

REGULAR

SAD

ANGRY

DAILY TRACKER

SLEEP

DATE _____   (M T W T F S

MY INTENTION FOR THE DAY IS

_____

_____

THIS IS HOW I WILL MAKE TODAY GREAT

_____

TOP THREE TASKS

○ _____

○ _____

○ _____

OTHER TASKS

○ _____
○ _____
○ _____
○ _____
○ _____
○ _____
○ _____
○ _____
○ _____
○ _____
○ _____
○ _____
○ _____

DAILY SCHEDULE

TIME	TASK

DAILY TRACKER

LAST NIGHT, I DREAMT

MY BEST THOUGHTS WERE

MY REWARD FOR MEETING MY GOALS IS

TODAY, I FEEL

EXCELLENT   GOOD   REGULAR   SAD   ANGRY

DAILY TRACKER

SLEEP

DATE _____

M T W T F S S

MY INTENTION FOR THE DAY IS

_____

_____

THIS IS HOW I WILL MAKE TODAY GREAT

_____

_____

TOP THREE TASKS

○ _____
○ _____
○ _____

OTHER TASKS

○ _____
○ _____
○ _____
○ _____
○ _____
○ _____
○ _____
○ _____
○ _____
○ _____
○ _____
○ _____
○ _____

DAILY SCHEDULE

TIME	TASK

DAILY TRACKER

LAST NIGHT, I DREAMT

MY BEST THOUGHTS WERE

MY REWARD FOR MEETING MY GOALS IS

TODAY, I FEEL

EXCELLENT

GOOD

REGULAR

SAD

ANGRY

DAILY TRACKER

SLEEP

month two.

RELAX YOUR SHOULDERS

MY HAPPIEST MEMORY THIS MONTH WAS

THIS MONTH, I WAS MOST PROUD OF

THIS MONTH, I LEARNT

MONTHLY REFLECTIONS

WHAT STRESS OR CONCERN WORKED ITSELF OUT?

WHAT DIDN'T GO TO PLAN? AND HOW CAN I IMPROVE IT?

WHAT AREAS OF MY LIFE DID I GROW THE MOST IN?

MON	TUE	WED	THU
————	————	————	————
————	————	————	————
————	————	————	————
————	————	————	————
————	————	————	————

IDEAS

NEXT MONTH'S OVERVIEW

FRI	SAT	SUN	
			NOTES

REFLECTIONS

DATE _____

MY INTENTION FOR THE DAY IS

_____

_____

THIS IS HOW I WILL MAKE TODAY GREAT

_____

_____

TOP THREE TASKS

○ _____

○ _____

○ _____

OTHER TASKS

○ _____
○ _____
○ _____
○ _____
○ _____
○ _____
○ _____
○ _____
○ _____
○ _____
○ _____
○ _____
○ _____

DAILY SCHEDULE

TIME	TASK

DAILY TRACKER

LAST NIGHT, I DREAMT

MY BEST THOUGHTS WERE

MY REWARD FOR MEETING MY GOALS IS

TODAY, I FEEL

EXCELLENT　　　GOOD　　　REGULAR　　　SAD　　　ANGRY

DAILY TRACKER

SLEEP

DATE _____

MY INTENTION FOR THE DAY IS

_____

_____

THIS IS HOW I WILL MAKE TODAY GREAT

_____

TOP THREE TASKS

O _____

O _____

O _____

OTHER TASKS

O _____

O _____

O _____

O _____

O _____

O _____

O _____

O _____

O _____

O _____

O _____

O _____

O _____

DAILY SCHEDULE

TIME	TASK

DAILY TRACKER

LAST NIGHT, I DREAMT

MY BEST THOUGHTS WERE

MY REWARD FOR MEETING MY GOALS IS

TODAY, I FEEL

EXCELLENT   GOOD   REGULAR   SAD   ANGRY

DAILY TRACKER

SLEEP

DATE _____

MY INTENTION FOR THE DAY IS

_____

_____

THIS IS HOW I WILL MAKE TODAY GREAT

_____

_____

TOP THREE TASKS

- ○ _____
- ○ _____
- ○ _____

OTHER TASKS

- ○ _____
- ○ _____
- ○ _____
- ○ _____
- ○ _____
- ○ _____
- ○ _____
- ○ _____
- ○ _____
- ○ _____
- ○ _____
- ○ _____
- ○ _____

DAILY SCHEDULE

TIME	TASK

DAILY TRACKER

LAST NIGHT, I DREAMT

_____

_____

_____

MY BEST THOUGHTS WERE

_____

_____

_____

MY REWARD FOR MEETING MY GOALS IS

_____

_____

_____

TODAY, I FEEL

EXCELLENT

GOOD

REGULAR

SAD

ANGRY

DAILY TRACKER

SLEEP

DATE _____

MY INTENTION FOR THE DAY IS

_____

_____

THIS IS HOW I WILL MAKE TODAY GREAT

_____

TOP THREE TASKS

- ○ _____
- ○ _____
- ○ _____

OTHER TASKS

- ○ _____
- ○ _____
- ○ _____
- ○ _____
- ○ _____
- ○ _____
- ○ _____
- ○ _____
- ○ _____
- ○ _____
- ○ _____
- ○ _____
- ○ _____

DAILY SCHEDULE

TIME	TASK

DAILY TRACKER

LAST NIGHT, I DREAMT

MY BEST THOUGHTS WERE

MY REWARD FOR MEETING MY GOALS IS

TODAY, I FEEL

EXCELLENT   GOOD   REGULAR   SAD   ANGRY

DAILY TRACKER

SLEEP

DATE _____

MY INTENTION FOR THE DAY IS

_____

_____

THIS IS HOW I WILL MAKE TODAY GREAT

_____

_____

TOP THREE TASKS

- ○ _____
- ○ _____
- ○ _____

OTHER TASKS

- ○ _____
- ○ _____
- ○ _____
- ○ _____
- ○ _____
- ○ _____
- ○ _____
- ○ _____
- ○ _____
- ○ _____
- ○ _____
- ○ _____
- ○ _____

DAILY SCHEDULE

TIME	TASK

DAILY TRACKER

LAST NIGHT, I DREAMT

MY BEST THOUGHTS WERE

MY REWARD FOR MEETING MY GOALS IS

TODAY, I FEEL

| EXCELLENT | GOOD | REGULAR | SAD | ANGRY |

DAILY TRACKER

SLEEP

DATE _____   (M T W T F S

MY INTENTION FOR THE DAY IS

_____

_____

THIS IS HOW I WILL MAKE TODAY GREAT

_____

_____

TOP THREE TASKS

- O _____
- O _____
- O _____

OTHER TASKS

- O _____
- O _____
- O _____
- O _____
- O _____
- O _____
- O _____
- O _____
- O _____
- O _____
- O _____
- O _____
- O _____

DAILY SCHEDULE

TIME	TASK

DAILY TRACKER

LAST NIGHT, I DREAMT

MY BEST THOUGHTS WERE

MY REWARD FOR MEETING MY GOALS IS

TODAY, I FEEL

EXCELLENT

GOOD

REGULAR

SAD

ANGRY

DAILY TRACKER

SLEEP

DATE _____

MY INTENTION FOR THE DAY IS

_____

_____

THIS IS HOW I WILL MAKE TODAY GREAT

_____

_____

TOP THREE TASKS

○ _____

○ _____

○ _____

OTHER TASKS

○ _____

○ _____

○ _____

○ _____

○ _____

○ _____

○ _____

○ _____

○ _____

○ _____

○ _____

○ _____

○ _____

DAILY SCHEDULE

TIME	TASK

DAILY TRACKER

LAST NIGHT, I DREAMT

_____

_____

_____

MY BEST THOUGHTS WERE

_____

_____

_____

MY REWARD FOR MEETING MY GOALS IS

_____

_____

_____

TODAY, I FEEL

| EXCELLENT | GOOD | REGULAR | SAD | ANGRY |

DAILY TRACKER

 SLEEP

I DREAM MY
PAINTING AND I
PAINT MY DREAM.

Vincent van Gogh

WEEKLY TRACKER

MY WEEKLY WINS

_____

_____

_____

_____

THIS WEEK, I LEARNT

_____

_____

_____

HABIT TRACKER

HABIT	M	T	W	T	F	S	S
	●	●	●	●	●	●	●
	●	●	●	●	●	●	●
	●	●	●	●	●	●	●

MY TASKS FOR NEXT WEEK

- ○ _____
- ○ _____
- ○ _____
- ○ _____
- ○ _____
- ○ _____
- ○ _____

DATE _____ 〔 M T W T F S S

MY INTENTION FOR THE DAY IS

_____

_____

THIS IS HOW I WILL MAKE TODAY GREAT

_____

_____

TOP THREE TASKS

- ○ _____
- ○ _____
- ○ _____

OTHER TASKS

- ○ _____
- ○ _____
- ○ _____
- ○ _____
- ○ _____
- ○ _____
- ○ _____
- ○ _____
- ○ _____
- ○ _____
- ○ _____
- ○ _____
- ○ _____

DAILY SCHEDULE

TIME	TASK

DAILY TRACKER

LAST NIGHT, I DREAMT

MY BEST THOUGHTS WERE

MY REWARD FOR MEETING MY GOALS IS

TODAY, I FEEL

EXCELLENT   GOOD   REGULAR   SAD   ANGRY

DAILY TRACKER

SLEEP

DATE _____   M T W T F S S

MY INTENTION FOR THE DAY IS

_____

_____

THIS IS HOW I WILL MAKE TODAY GREAT

_____

TOP THREE TASKS

O _____

O _____

O _____

OTHER TASKS

O _____

O _____

O _____

O _____

O _____

O _____

O _____

O _____

O _____

O _____

O _____

O _____

O _____

DAILY SCHEDULE

TIME	TASK

DAILY TRACKER

LAST NIGHT, I DREAMT

MY BEST THOUGHTS WERE

MY REWARD FOR MEETING MY GOALS IS

TODAY, I FEEL

EXCELLENT   GOOD   REGULAR   SAD   ANGRY

DAILY TRACKER

 SLEEP

DATE _____

M T W T F S

MY INTENTION FOR THE DAY IS

_____

_____

THIS IS HOW I WILL MAKE TODAY GREAT

_____

TOP THREE TASKS

- ◯ _____
- ◯ _____
- ◯ _____

OTHER TASKS

- ◯ _____
- ◯ _____
- ◯ _____
- ◯ _____
- ◯ _____
- ◯ _____
- ◯ _____
- ◯ _____
- ◯ _____
- ◯ _____
- ◯ _____
- ◯ _____
- ◯ _____

DAILY SCHEDULE

TIME	TASK

DAILY TRACKER

LAST NIGHT, I DREAMT

MY BEST THOUGHTS WERE

MY REWARD FOR MEETING MY GOALS IS

TODAY, I FEEL

EXCELLENT

GOOD

REGULAR

SAD

ANGRY

DAILY TRACKER

SLEEP

DATE _____   (M T W T F S S

MY INTENTION FOR THE DAY IS

_____

_____

THIS IS HOW I WILL MAKE TODAY GREAT

_____

TOP THREE TASKS

○ _____
○ _____
○ _____

OTHER TASKS

○ _____
○ _____
○ _____
○ _____
○ _____
○ _____
○ _____
○ _____
○ _____
○ _____
○ _____
○ _____
○ _____

DAILY SCHEDULE

TIME	TASK

DAILY TRACKER

LAST NIGHT, I DREAMT

_____

_____

_____

MY BEST THOUGHTS WERE

_____

_____

_____

MY REWARD FOR MEETING MY GOALS IS

_____

_____

_____

TODAY, I FEEL

EXCELLENT

GOOD

REGULAR

SAD

ANGRY

DAILY TRACKER

SLEEP

DATE _____ (M T W T F S S

MY INTENTION FOR THE DAY IS

_____

_____

THIS IS HOW I WILL MAKE TODAY GREAT

_____

TOP THREE TASKS

- ◯ _____
- ◯ _____
- ◯ _____

OTHER TASKS

- ◯ _____
- ◯ _____
- ◯ _____
- ◯ _____
- ◯ _____
- ◯ _____
- ◯ _____
- ◯ _____
- ◯ _____
- ◯ _____
- ◯ _____
- ◯ _____
- ◯ _____

DAILY SCHEDULE

TIME	TASK

DAILY TRACKER

LAST NIGHT, I DREAMT

_____

_____

_____

MY BEST THOUGHTS WERE

_____

_____

_____

MY REWARD FOR MEETING MY GOALS IS

_____

_____

TODAY, I FEEL

EXCELLENT   GOOD   REGULAR   SAD   ANGRY

DAILY TRACKER

SLEEP

DATE _____

MY INTENTION FOR THE DAY IS

_____

_____

THIS IS HOW I WILL MAKE TODAY GREAT

_____

TOP THREE TASKS

- ○ _____
- ○ _____
- ○ _____

OTHER TASKS

- ○ _____
- ○ _____
- ○ _____
- ○ _____
- ○ _____
- ○ _____
- ○ _____
- ○ _____
- ○ _____
- ○ _____
- ○ _____
- ○ _____
- ○ _____

DAILY SCHEDULE

TIME	TASK

DAILY TRACKER

LAST NIGHT, I DREAMT

MY BEST THOUGHTS WERE

MY REWARD FOR MEETING MY GOALS IS

TODAY, I FEEL

EXCELLENT   GOOD   REGULAR   SAD   ANGRY

DAILY TRACKER

SLEEP

DATE _____   (M T W T F S S

MY INTENTION FOR THE DAY IS

_____

_____

THIS IS HOW I WILL MAKE TODAY GREAT

_____

_____

TOP THREE TASKS

- O _____
- O _____
- O _____

OTHER TASKS

- O _____
- O _____
- O _____
- O _____
- O _____
- O _____
- O _____
- O _____
- O _____
- O _____
- O _____
- O _____
- O _____

DAILY SCHEDULE

TIME	TASK

DAILY TRACKER

LAST NIGHT, I DREAMT

MY BEST THOUGHTS WERE

MY REWARD FOR MEETING MY GOALS IS

TODAY, I FEEL

EXCELLENT	GOOD	REGULAR	SAD	ANGRY

DAILY TRACKER

SLEEP

REAL GENEROSITY
TOWARDS THE FUTURE
LIES IN GIVING ALL TO
THE PRESENT.

Albert Camus

WEEKLY TRACKER

MY WEEKLY WINS

THIS WEEK, I LEARNT

HABIT TRACKER

HABIT	M	T	W	T	F	S	S
	●	●	●	●	●	●	●
	●	●	●	●	●	●	●
	●	●	●	●	●	●	●

MY TASKS FOR NEXT WEEK

- ○
- ○
- ○
- ○
- ○
- ○
- ○

DATE _____   (M T W T F S S

MY INTENTION FOR THE DAY IS

_____

_____

THIS IS HOW I WILL MAKE TODAY GREAT

_____

_____

TOP THREE TASKS

O _____

O _____

O _____

OTHER TASKS

O _____
O _____
O _____
O _____
O _____
O _____
O _____
O _____
O _____
O _____
O _____
O _____
O _____

DAILY SCHEDULE

TIME	TASK

DAILY TRACKER

LAST NIGHT, I DREAMT

MY BEST THOUGHTS WERE

MY REWARD FOR MEETING MY GOALS IS

TODAY, I FEEL

EXCELLENT   GOOD   REGULAR   SAD   ANGRY

DAILY TRACKER

SLEEP

DATE _____

MY INTENTION FOR THE DAY IS

_____

_____

THIS IS HOW I WILL MAKE TODAY GREAT

_____

TOP THREE TASKS

○ _____
○ _____
○ _____

OTHER TASKS

○ _____
○ _____
○ _____
○ _____
○ _____
○ _____
○ _____
○ _____
○ _____
○ _____
○ _____
○ _____
○ _____

DAILY SCHEDULE

TIME	TASK

DAILY TRACKER

LAST NIGHT, I DREAMT

_____

_____

_____

MY BEST THOUGHTS WERE

_____

_____

_____

MY REWARD FOR MEETING MY GOALS IS

_____

_____

_____

TODAY, I FEEL

EXCELLENT   GOOD   REGULAR   SAD   ANGRY

DAILY TRACKER

SLEEP

DATE _____

MY INTENTION FOR THE DAY IS

_____

_____

THIS IS HOW I WILL MAKE TODAY GREAT

_____

TOP THREE TASKS

○ _____

○ _____

○ _____

OTHER TASKS

○ _____
○ _____
○ _____
○ _____
○ _____
○ _____
○ _____
○ _____
○ _____
○ _____
○ _____
○ _____
○ _____

DAILY SCHEDULE

TIME	TASK

DAILY TRACKER

LAST NIGHT, I DREAMT

MY BEST THOUGHTS WERE

MY REWARD FOR MEETING MY GOALS IS

TODAY, I FEEL

EXCELLENT

GOOD

REGULAR

SAD

ANGRY

DAILY TRACKER

SLEEP

DATE _____

MY INTENTION FOR THE DAY IS

_____

_____

THIS IS HOW I WILL MAKE TODAY GREAT

_____

TOP THREE TASKS

○ _____

○ _____

○ _____

OTHER TASKS

○ _____
○ _____
○ _____
○ _____
○ _____
○ _____
○ _____
○ _____
○ _____
○ _____
○ _____
○ _____

DAILY SCHEDULE

TIME	TASK

DAILY TRACKER

LAST NIGHT, I DREAMT

MY BEST THOUGHTS WERE

MY REWARD FOR MEETING MY GOALS IS

TODAY, I FEEL

EXCELLENT

GOOD

REGULAR

SAD

ANGRY

DAILY TRACKER

SLEEP

DATE _____

MY INTENTION FOR THE DAY IS

_____

_____

THIS IS HOW I WILL MAKE TODAY GREAT

_____

_____

TOP THREE TASKS

- ◯ _____
- ◯ _____
- ◯ _____

OTHER TASKS

- ◯ _____
- ◯ _____
- ◯ _____
- ◯ _____
- ◯ _____
- ◯ _____
- ◯ _____
- ◯ _____
- ◯ _____
- ◯ _____
- ◯ _____
- ◯ _____
- ◯ _____

DAILY SCHEDULE

TIME	TASK

DAILY TRACKER

LAST NIGHT, I DREAMT

MY BEST THOUGHTS WERE

MY REWARD FOR MEETING MY GOALS IS

TODAY, I FEEL

EXCELLENT	GOOD	REGULAR	SAD	ANGRY

DAILY TRACKER

SLEEP

DATE _____   (M T W T F S S)

MY INTENTION FOR THE DAY IS

_____

_____

THIS IS HOW I WILL MAKE TODAY GREAT

_____

TOP THREE TASKS

○ _____

○ _____

○ _____

OTHER TASKS

○ _____

○ _____

○ _____

○ _____

○ _____

○ _____

○ _____

○ _____

○ _____

○ _____

○ _____

○ _____

○ _____

DAILY SCHEDULE

TIME	TASK

DAILY TRACKER

LAST NIGHT, I DREAMT

MY BEST THOUGHTS WERE

MY REWARD FOR MEETING MY GOALS IS

TODAY, I FEEL

| EXCELLENT | GOOD | REGULAR | SAD | ANGRY |

DAILY TRACKER

SLEEP

DATE _____   (M T W T F S S)

MY INTENTION FOR THE DAY IS

_____

_____

THIS IS HOW I WILL MAKE TODAY GREAT

_____

TOP THREE TASKS

- ○ _____
- ○ _____
- ○ _____

OTHER TASKS

- ○ _____
- ○ _____
- ○ _____
- ○ _____
- ○ _____
- ○ _____
- ○ _____
- ○ _____
- ○ _____
- ○ _____
- ○ _____
- ○ _____

DAILY SCHEDULE

TIME	TASK

DAILY TRACKER

LAST NIGHT, I DREAMT

_____

_____

_____

MY BEST THOUGHTS WERE

_____

_____

_____

MY REWARD FOR MEETING MY GOALS IS

_____

_____

_____

TODAY, I FEEL

EXCELLENT

GOOD

REGULAR

SAD

ANGRY

DAILY TRACKER

SLEEP

DON'T COUNT THE DAYS, MAKE THE DAYS COUNT.

Muhammad Ali

WEEKLY TRACKER

MY WEEKLY WINS

THIS WEEK, I LEARNT

HABIT TRACKER

HABIT	M	T	W	T	F	S	S
	●	●	●	●	●	●	●
	●	●	●	●	●	●	●
	●	●	●	●	●	●	●

MY TASKS FOR NEXT WEEK

○
○
○
○
○
○
○

DATE _____   (M T W T F S S

MY INTENTION FOR THE DAY IS

_____

_____

THIS IS HOW I WILL MAKE TODAY GREAT

_____

TOP THREE TASKS

- ○ _____
- ○ _____
- ○ _____

OTHER TASKS

- ○ _____
- ○ _____
- ○ _____
- ○ _____
- ○ _____
- ○ _____
- ○ _____
- ○ _____
- ○ _____
- ○ _____
- ○ _____
- ○ _____
- ○ _____

DAILY SCHEDULE

TIME	TASK

DAILY TRACKER

LAST NIGHT, I DREAMT

MY BEST THOUGHTS WERE

MY REWARD FOR MEETING MY GOALS IS

TODAY, I FEEL

EXCELLENT   GOOD   REGULAR   SAD   ANGRY

DAILY TRACKER

SLEEP

DATE _____

MY INTENTION FOR THE DAY IS

_____

_____

THIS IS HOW I WILL MAKE TODAY GREAT

_____

TOP THREE TASKS

O _____

O _____

O _____

OTHER TASKS

O _____

O _____

O _____

O _____

O _____

O _____

O _____

O _____

O _____

O _____

O _____

O _____

O _____

DAILY SCHEDULE

TIME	TASK

DAILY TRACKER

LAST NIGHT, I DREAMT

MY BEST THOUGHTS WERE

MY REWARD FOR MEETING MY GOALS IS

TODAY, I FEEL

| EXCELLENT | GOOD | REGULAR | SAD | ANGRY |

DAILY TRACKER

SLEEP

M T W T F S

MY INTENTION FOR THE DAY IS

_____

_____

THIS IS HOW I WILL MAKE TODAY GREAT

_____

TOP THREE TASKS

○ _____
○ _____
○ _____

OTHER TASKS

○ _____
○ _____
○ _____
○ _____
○ _____
○ _____
○ _____
○ _____
○ _____
○ _____
○ _____
○ _____
○ _____

DAILY SCHEDULE

TIME	TASK

DAILY TRACKER

LAST NIGHT, I DREAMT

MY BEST THOUGHTS WERE

MY REWARD FOR MEETING MY GOALS IS

TODAY, I FEEL

EXCELLENT   GOOD   REGULAR   SAD   ANGRY

DAILY TRACKER

SLEEP

DATE _____   (M T W T F S

MY INTENTION FOR THE DAY IS

_____

_____

THIS IS HOW I WILL MAKE TODAY GREAT

_____

TOP THREE TASKS

○ _____

○ _____

○ _____

OTHER TASKS

○ _____
○ _____
○ _____
○ _____
○ _____
○ _____
○ _____
○ _____
○ _____
○ _____
○ _____
○ _____
○ _____

DAILY SCHEDULE

TIME	TASK

DAILY TRACKER

LAST NIGHT, I DREAMT

MY BEST THOUGHTS WERE

MY REWARD FOR MEETING MY GOALS IS

TODAY, I FEEL

EXCELLENT   GOOD   REGULAR   SAD   ANGRY

DAILY TRACKER

SLEEP

DATE _____   (M T W T F S S

MY INTENTION FOR THE DAY IS

_____

_____

THIS IS HOW I WILL MAKE TODAY GREAT

_____

TOP THREE TASKS

- ○ _____
- ○ _____
- ○ _____

OTHER TASKS

- ○ _____
- ○ _____
- ○ _____
- ○ _____
- ○ _____
- ○ _____
- ○ _____
- ○ _____
- ○ _____
- ○ _____
- ○ _____
- ○ _____
- ○ _____

DAILY SCHEDULE

TIME	TASK

DAILY TRACKER

LAST NIGHT, I DREAMT

_____

_____

_____

MY BEST THOUGHTS WERE

_____

_____

_____

MY REWARD FOR MEETING MY GOALS IS

_____

_____

_____

TODAY, I FEEL

| EXCELLENT | GOOD | REGULAR | SAD | ANGRY |

DAILY TRACKER

SLEEP

DATE _____

M T W T F S

MY INTENTION FOR THE DAY IS

_____

_____

THIS IS HOW I WILL MAKE TODAY GREAT

_____

TOP THREE TASKS

○ _____

○ _____

○ _____

OTHER TASKS

○ _____

○ _____

○ _____

○ _____

○ _____

○ _____

○ _____

○ _____

○ _____

○ _____

○ _____

○ _____

○ _____

DAILY SCHEDULE

TIME	TASK

DAILY TRACKER

LAST NIGHT, I DREAMT

MY BEST THOUGHTS WERE

MY REWARD FOR MEETING MY GOALS IS

TODAY, I FEEL

EXCELLENT   GOOD   REGULAR   SAD   ANGRY

DAILY TRACKER

SLEEP

DATE _____

MY INTENTION FOR THE DAY IS

_____

_____

THIS IS HOW I WILL MAKE TODAY GREAT

_____

TOP THREE TASKS

- ○ _____
- ○ _____
- ○ _____

OTHER TASKS

- ○ _____
- ○ _____
- ○ _____
- ○ _____
- ○ _____
- ○ _____
- ○ _____
- ○ _____
- ○ _____
- ○ _____
- ○ _____
- ○ _____
- ○ _____

DAILY SCHEDULE

TIME	TASK

DAILY TRACKER

LAST NIGHT, I DREAMT

MY BEST THOUGHTS WERE

MY REWARD FOR MEETING MY GOALS IS

TODAY, I FEEL

EXCELLENT   GOOD   REGULAR   SAD   ANGRY

DAILY TRACKER

SLEEP

I BELIEVE GREAT
ART IS DISCOVERED
WHEN YOU ARE
CONSISTENT.

Beyoncé Giselle Knowles-Carter

bonus days.

TAKE TIME

DATE _____

MY INTENTION FOR THE DAY IS

_____

_____

THIS IS HOW I WILL MAKE TODAY GREAT

_____

_____

TOP THREE TASKS

- ◯ _____
- ◯ _____
- ◯ _____

OTHER TASKS

- ◯ _____
- ◯ _____
- ◯ _____
- ◯ _____
- ◯ _____
- ◯ _____
- ◯ _____
- ◯ _____
- ◯ _____
- ◯ _____
- ◯ _____
- ◯ _____
- ◯ _____

DAILY SCHEDULE

TIME	TASK

DAILY TRACKER

LAST NIGHT, I DREAMT

MY BEST THOUGHTS WERE

MY REWARD FOR MEETING MY GOALS IS

TODAY, I FEEL

EXCELLENT	GOOD	REGULAR	SAD	ANGRY

DAILY TRACKER

SLEEP

DATE _____

MY INTENTION FOR THE DAY IS

_____

_____

THIS IS HOW I WILL MAKE TODAY GREAT

_____

TOP THREE TASKS

○ _____

○ _____

○ _____

OTHER TASKS

○ _____
○ _____
○ _____
○ _____
○ _____
○ _____
○ _____
○ _____
○ _____
○ _____
○ _____
○ _____
○ _____

DAILY SCHEDULE

TIME	TASK

DAILY TRACKER

LAST NIGHT, I DREAMT

MY BEST THOUGHTS WERE

MY REWARD FOR MEETING MY GOALS IS

TODAY, I FEEL

EXCELLENT   GOOD   REGULAR   SAD   ANGRY

DAILY TRACKER

SLEEP

DATE _____

MY INTENTION FOR THE DAY IS

_____

_____

THIS IS HOW I WILL MAKE TODAY GREAT

_____

_____

TOP THREE TASKS

○ _____
○ _____
○ _____

OTHER TASKS

○ _____
○ _____
○ _____
○ _____
○ _____
○ _____
○ _____
○ _____
○ _____
○ _____
○ _____
○ _____
○ _____

DAILY SCHEDULE

TIME	TASK

DAILY TRACKER

LAST NIGHT, I DREAMT

MY BEST THOUGHTS WERE

MY REWARD FOR MEETING MY GOALS IS

TODAY, I FEEL

EXCELLENT

GOOD

REGULAR

SAD

ANGRY

DAILY TRACKER

SLEEP

month three.

SETTLE INTO YOURSELF

MY HAPPIEST MEMORY THIS MONTH WAS

THIS MONTH, I WAS MOST PROUD OF

THIS MONTH, I LEARNT

MONTHLY REFLECTIONS

WHAT STRESS OR CONCERN WORKED ITSELF OUT?

WHAT DIDN'T GO TO PLAN? AND HOW CAN I IMPROVE IT?

WHAT AREAS OF MY LIFE DID I GROW THE MOST IN?

MON	TUE	WED	THU

IDEAS

NEXT MONTH'S OVERVIEW

FRI　　　　　　　　SAT　　　　　　　SUN

NOTES

REFLECTIONS

DATE _____   (M T W T F S S)

MY INTENTION FOR THE DAY IS

_____

_____

THIS IS HOW I WILL MAKE TODAY GREAT

_____

_____

TOP THREE TASKS

- ○ _____
- ○ _____
- ○ _____

OTHER TASKS

- ○ _____
- ○ _____
- ○ _____
- ○ _____
- ○ _____
- ○ _____
- ○ _____
- ○ _____
- ○ _____
- ○ _____
- ○ _____
- ○ _____

DAILY SCHEDULE

TIME	TASK

DAILY TRACKER

LAST NIGHT, I DREAMT

_____

_____

_____

MY BEST THOUGHTS WERE

_____

_____

_____

MY REWARD FOR MEETING MY GOALS IS

_____

_____

_____

TODAY, I FEEL

EXCELLENT

GOOD

REGULAR

SAD

ANGRY

DAILY TRACKER

  SLEEP

DATE _____

MY INTENTION FOR THE DAY IS

_____

_____

THIS IS HOW I WILL MAKE TODAY GREAT

_____

TOP THREE TASKS

○ _____

○ _____

○ _____

OTHER TASKS

○ _____
○ _____
○ _____
○ _____
○ _____
○ _____
○ _____
○ _____
○ _____
○ _____
○ _____
○ _____
○ _____

DAILY SCHEDULE

TIME	TASK

DAILY TRACKER

LAST NIGHT, I DREAMT

MY BEST THOUGHTS WERE

MY REWARD FOR MEETING MY GOALS IS

TODAY, I FEEL

EXCELLENT

GOOD

REGULAR

SAD

ANGRY

DAILY TRACKER

SLEEP

DATE _____

MY INTENTION FOR THE DAY IS

_____

_____

THIS IS HOW I WILL MAKE TODAY GREAT

_____

_____

TOP THREE TASKS

- ○ _____
- ○ _____
- ○ _____

OTHER TASKS

- ○ _____
- ○ _____
- ○ _____
- ○ _____
- ○ _____
- ○ _____
- ○ _____
- ○ _____
- ○ _____
- ○ _____
- ○ _____
- ○ _____
- ○ _____

DAILY SCHEDULE

TIME	TASK

DAILY TRACKER

LAST NIGHT, I DREAMT

MY BEST THOUGHTS WERE

MY REWARD FOR MEETING MY GOALS IS

TODAY, I FEEL

EXCELLENT

GOOD

REGULAR

SAD

ANGRY

DAILY TRACKER

SLEEP

DATE _____   (M T W T F S

MY INTENTION FOR THE DAY IS

_____

_____

THIS IS HOW I WILL MAKE TODAY GREAT

_____

TOP THREE TASKS

- ○ _____
- ○ _____
- ○ _____

OTHER TASKS

- ○ _____
- ○ _____
- ○ _____
- ○ _____
- ○ _____
- ○ _____
- ○ _____
- ○ _____
- ○ _____
- ○ _____
- ○ _____
- ○ _____
- ○ _____

DAILY SCHEDULE

TIME	TASK

DAILY TRACKER

LAST NIGHT, I DREAMT

MY BEST THOUGHTS WERE

MY REWARD FOR MEETING MY GOALS IS

TODAY, I FEEL

EXCELLENT   GOOD   REGULAR   SAD   ANGRY

DAILY TRACKER

SLEEP

DATE _____   (M T W T F S)

MY INTENTION FOR THE DAY IS

_____

_____

THIS IS HOW I WILL MAKE TODAY GREAT

_____

_____

TOP THREE TASKS

- ○ _____
- ○ _____
- ○ _____

OTHER TASKS

- ○ _____
- ○ _____
- ○ _____
- ○ _____
- ○ _____
- ○ _____
- ○ _____
- ○ _____
- ○ _____
- ○ _____
- ○ _____
- ○ _____
- ○ _____

DAILY SCHEDULE

TIME	TASK

DAILY TRACKER

LAST NIGHT, I DREAMT

_____

_____

_____

MY BEST THOUGHTS WERE

_____

_____

_____

MY REWARD FOR MEETING MY GOALS IS

_____

_____

_____

TODAY, I FEEL

EXCELLENT   GOOD   REGULAR   SAD   ANGRY

DAILY TRACKER

SLEEP

175

DATE _____   M T W T F S

MY INTENTION FOR THE DAY IS

_____

_____

THIS IS HOW I WILL MAKE TODAY GREAT

_____

TOP THREE TASKS

○ _____

○ _____

○ _____

OTHER TASKS

○ _____
○ _____
○ _____
○ _____
○ _____
○ _____
○ _____
○ _____
○ _____
○ _____
○ _____
○ _____
○ _____

DAILY SCHEDULE

TIME	TASK

DAILY TRACKER

LAST NIGHT, I DREAMT

MY BEST THOUGHTS WERE

MY REWARD FOR MEETING MY GOALS IS

TODAY, I FEEL

EXCELLENT

GOOD

REGULAR

SAD

ANGRY

DAILY TRACKER

SLEEP

DATE _____   (M T W T F S S

MY INTENTION FOR THE DAY IS

_____

_____

THIS IS HOW I WILL MAKE TODAY GREAT

_____

_____

TOP THREE TASKS

- ◯ _____
- ◯ _____
- ◯ _____

OTHER TASKS

- ◯ _____
- ◯ _____
- ◯ _____
- ◯ _____
- ◯ _____
- ◯ _____
- ◯ _____
- ◯ _____
- ◯ _____
- ◯ _____
- ◯ _____
- ◯ _____
- ◯ _____

DAILY SCHEDULE

TIME	TASK

DAILY TRACKER

LAST NIGHT, I DREAMT

MY BEST THOUGHTS WERE

MY REWARD FOR MEETING MY GOALS IS

TODAY, I FEEL

EXCELLENT   GOOD   REGULAR   SAD   ANGRY

DAILY TRACKER

SLEEP

START WHERE YOU ARE.
USE WHAT YOU HAVE.
DO WHAT YOU CAN.

Arthur Ashe

WEEKLY TRACKER

MY WEEKLY WINS

THIS WEEK, I LEARNT

HABIT TRACKER

HABIT	M	T	W	T	F	S	S
	○	○	○	○	○	○	○
	○	○	○	○	○	○	○
	○	○	○	○	○	○	○

MY TASKS FOR NEXT WEEK

○
○
○
○
○
○
○

DATE _____   M T W T F S S

MY INTENTION FOR THE DAY IS

_____

_____

THIS IS HOW I WILL MAKE TODAY GREAT

_____

_____

TOP THREE TASKS

- ◯ _____
- ◯ _____
- ◯ _____

OTHER TASKS

- ◯ _____
- ◯ _____
- ◯ _____
- ◯ _____
- ◯ _____
- ◯ _____
- ◯ _____
- ◯ _____
- ◯ _____
- ◯ _____
- ◯ _____
- ◯ _____
- ◯ _____

DAILY SCHEDULE

TIME	TASK

DAILY TRACKER

LAST NIGHT, I DREAMT

MY BEST THOUGHTS WERE

MY REWARD FOR MEETING MY GOALS IS

TODAY, I FEEL

EXCELLENT   GOOD   REGULAR   SAD   ANGRY

DAILY TRACKER

SLEEP

DATE _____

MY INTENTION FOR THE DAY IS

_____

_____

THIS IS HOW I WILL MAKE TODAY GREAT

_____

_____

TOP THREE TASKS

O _____
O _____
O _____

OTHER TASKS

O _____
O _____
O _____
O _____
O _____
O _____
O _____
O _____
O _____
O _____
O _____
O _____
O _____

DAILY SCHEDULE

TIME	TASK

DAILY TRACKER

LAST NIGHT, I DREAMT

_____

_____

_____

MY BEST THOUGHTS WERE

_____

_____

_____

MY REWARD FOR MEETING MY GOALS IS

_____

_____

_____

TODAY, I FEEL

| EXCELLENT | GOOD | REGULAR | SAD | ANGRY |

DAILY TRACKER

SLEEP

DATE _____

MY INTENTION FOR THE DAY IS

_____

_____

THIS IS HOW I WILL MAKE TODAY GREAT

_____

TOP THREE TASKS

O _____

O _____

O _____

OTHER TASKS

O _____
O _____
O _____
O _____
O _____
O _____
O _____
O _____
O _____
O _____
O _____
O _____
O _____

DAILY SCHEDULE

TIME	TASK

DAILY TRACKER

LAST NIGHT, I DREAMT

MY BEST THOUGHTS WERE

MY REWARD FOR MEETING MY GOALS IS

TODAY, I FEEL

EXCELLENT	GOOD	REGULAR	SAD	ANGRY

DAILY TRACKER

DATE _____

MY INTENTION FOR THE DAY IS

_____

_____

THIS IS HOW I WILL MAKE TODAY GREAT

_____

TOP THREE TASKS

- ○ _____
- ○ _____
- ○ _____

OTHER TASKS

- ○ _____
- ○ _____
- ○ _____
- ○ _____
- ○ _____
- ○ _____
- ○ _____
- ○ _____
- ○ _____
- ○ _____
- ○ _____
- ○ _____
- ○ _____

DAILY SCHEDULE

TIME	TASK

DAILY TRACKER

MY BEST THOUGHTS WERE

LAST NIGHT, I DREAMT

MY BEST THOUGHTS WERE

MY REWARD FOR MEETING MY GOALS IS

TODAY, I FEEL

EXCELLENT

GOOD

REGULAR

SAD

ANGRY

DAILY TRACKER

SLEEP

DATE _____ (M T W T F S S

MY INTENTION FOR THE DAY IS

_____

_____

THIS IS HOW I WILL MAKE TODAY GREAT

_____

TOP THREE TASKS

- O _____
- O _____
- O _____

OTHER TASKS

- O _____
- O _____
- O _____
- O _____
- O _____
- O _____
- O _____
- O _____
- O _____
- O _____
- O _____
- O _____
- O _____

DAILY SCHEDULE

TIME	TASK

DAILY TRACKER

LAST NIGHT, I DREAMT

MY BEST THOUGHTS WERE

MY REWARD FOR MEETING MY GOALS IS

TODALY, I FEEL

EXCELLENT	GOOD	REGULAR	SAD	ANGRY

DAILY TRACKER

SLEEP

DATE _____

MY INTENTION FOR THE DAY IS

_____

_____

THIS IS HOW I WILL MAKE TODAY GREAT

_____

_____

TOP THREE TASKS

- ○ _____
- ○ _____
- ○ _____

OTHER TASKS

- ○ _____
- ○ _____
- ○ _____
- ○ _____
- ○ _____
- ○ _____
- ○ _____
- ○ _____
- ○ _____
- ○ _____
- ○ _____
- ○ _____
- ○ _____

DAILY SCHEDULE

TIME	TASK

DAILY TRACKER

LAST NIGHT, I DREAMT

MY BEST THOUGHTS WERE

MY REWARD FOR MEETING MY GOALS IS

TODAY, I FEEL

EXCELLENT   GOOD   REGULAR   SAD   ANGRY

DAILY TRACKER

SLEEP

DATE _____   (M T W T F S S

MY INTENTION FOR THE DAY IS

_____

_____

THIS IS HOW I WILL MAKE TODAY GREAT

_____

TOP THREE TASKS

- ○ _____
- ○ _____
- ○ _____

OTHER TASKS

- ○ _____
- ○ _____
- ○ _____
- ○ _____
- ○ _____
- ○ _____
- ○ _____
- ○ _____
- ○ _____
- ○ _____
- ○ _____
- ○ _____
- ○ _____

DAILY SCHEDULE

TIME	TASK

DAILY TRACKER

LAST NIGHT, I DREAMT

MY BEST THOUGHTS WERE

MY REWARD FOR MEETING MY GOALS IS

TODAY, I FEEL

| EXCELLENT | GOOD | REGULAR | SAD | ANGRY |

DAILY TRACKER

SLEEP

WHAT'S THE WORLD
FOR IF YOU CAN'T
MAKE IT UP THE WAY
YOU WANT IT?

Toni Morrison

WEEKLY TRACKER

MY WEEKLY WINS

THIS WEEK, I LEARNT

HABIT TRACKER

HABIT	M	T	W	T	F	S	S
	●	●	●	●	●	●	●
	●	●	●	●	●	●	●
	●	●	●	●	●	●	●

MY TASKS FOR NEXT WEEK

○
○
○
○
○
○
○

DATE _____

MY INTENTION FOR THE DAY IS

_____

_____

THIS IS HOW I WILL MAKE TODAY GREAT

_____

_____

TOP THREE TASKS

- ○ _____
- ○ _____
- ○ _____

OTHER TASKS

- ○ _____
- ○ _____
- ○ _____
- ○ _____
- ○ _____
- ○ _____
- ○ _____
- ○ _____
- ○ _____
- ○ _____
- ○ _____
- ○ _____

DAILY SCHEDULE

TIME	TASK

DAILY TRACKER

LAST NIGHT, I DREAMT

MY BEST THOUGHTS WERE

MY REWARD FOR MEETING MY GOALS IS

TODAY, I FEEL

EXCELLENT

GOOD

REGULAR

SAD

ANGRY

DAILY TRACKER

SLEEP

DATE _____   (M T W T F S S

_____

_____

THIS IS HOW I WILL MAKE TODAY GREAT

_____

_____

TOP THREE TASKS

○ _____

○ _____

○ _____

OTHER TASKS

○ _____
○ _____
○ _____
○ _____
○ _____
○ _____
○ _____
○ _____
○ _____
○ _____
○ _____
○ _____
○ _____

DAILY SCHEDULE

TIME	TASK

DAILY TRACKER

LAST NIGHT, I DREAMT

_____

_____

_____

MY BEST THOUGHTS WERE

_____

_____

_____

MY REWARD FOR MEETING MY GOALS IS

_____

_____

_____

TODAY, I FEEL

EXCELLENT

GOOD

REGULAR

SAD

ANGRY

DAILY TRACKER

SLEEP

DATE _____

MY INTENTION FOR THE DAY IS

_____

_____

THIS IS HOW I WILL MAKE TODAY GREAT

_____

TOP THREE TASKS

- ◯ _____
- ◯ _____
- ◯ _____

OTHER TASKS

- ◯ _____
- ◯ _____
- ◯ _____
- ◯ _____
- ◯ _____
- ◯ _____
- ◯ _____
- ◯ _____
- ◯ _____
- ◯ _____
- ◯ _____
- ◯ _____
- ◯ _____

DAILY SCHEDULE

TIME	TASK

DAILY TRACKER

LAST NIGHT, I DREAMT

MY BEST THOUGHTS WERE

MY REWARD FOR MEETING MY GOALS IS

TODAY, I FEEL

EXCELLENT

GOOD

REGULAR

SAD

ANGRY

DAILY TRACKER

SLEEP

DATE _____

MY INTENTION FOR THE DAY IS

_____

_____

THIS IS HOW I WILL MAKE TODAY GREAT

_____

_____

TOP THREE TASKS

- ○ _____
- ○ _____
- ○ _____

OTHER TASKS

- ○ _____
- ○ _____
- ○ _____
- ○ _____
- ○ _____
- ○ _____
- ○ _____
- ○ _____
- ○ _____
- ○ _____
- ○ _____
- ○ _____

DAILY SCHEDULE

TIME	TASK

DAILY TRACKER

LAST NIGHT, I DREAMT

_____

_____

_____

MY BEST THOUGHTS WERE

_____

_____

_____

MY REWARD FOR MEETING MY GOALS IS

_____

_____

_____

TODAY, I FEEL

EXCELLENT   GOOD   REGULAR   SAD   ANGRY

DAILY TRACKER

SLEEP

DATE _____   M T W T F S

MY INTENTION FOR THE DAY IS

_____

_____

THIS IS HOW I WILL MAKE TODAY GREAT

_____

_____

TOP THREE TASKS

- O _____
- O _____
- O _____

OTHER TASKS

- O _____
- O _____
- O _____
- O _____
- O _____
- O _____
- O _____
- O _____
- O _____
- O _____
- O _____
- O _____
- O _____

DAILY SCHEDULE

TIME	TASK

DAILY TRACKER

LAST NIGHT, I DREAMT

_____

_____

_____

MY BEST THOUGHTS WERE

_____

_____

_____

MY REWARD FOR MEETING MY GOALS IS

_____

_____

_____

TODAY, I FEEL

EXCELLENT   GOOD   REGULAR   SAD   ANGRY

DAILY TRACKER

SLEEP

DATE _____

MY INTENTION FOR THE DAY IS

_____

_____

THIS IS HOW I WILL MAKE TODAY GREAT

_____

_____

TOP THREE TASKS

O _____

O _____

O _____

OTHER TASKS

O _____

O _____

O _____

O _____

O _____

O _____

O _____

O _____

O _____

O _____

O _____

O _____

O _____

DAILY SCHEDULE

TIME	TASK

DAILY TRACKER

LAST NIGHT, I DREAMT

MY BEST THOUGHTS WERE

MY REWARD FOR MEETING MY GOALS IS

TODAY, I FEEL

EXCELLENT   GOOD   REGULAR   SAD   ANGRY

DAILY TRACKER

SLEEP

DATE _____   (M T W T F S :

MY INTENTION FOR THE DAY IS

_____

_____

THIS IS HOW I WILL MAKE TODAY GREAT

_____

TOP THREE TASKS

- ○ _____
- ○ _____
- ○ _____

OTHER TASKS

- ○ _____
- ○ _____
- ○ _____
- ○ _____
- ○ _____
- ○ _____
- ○ _____
- ○ _____
- ○ _____
- ○ _____
- ○ _____
- ○ _____

DAILY SCHEDULE

TIME	TASK

DAILY TRACKER

MY BEST THOUGHTS WERE

MY REWARD FOR MEETING MY GOALS IS

TODDAY, I FEEL

EXCELLENT   GOOD   REGULAR   SAD   ANGRY

DAILY TRACKER

SLEEP

THINK OF MANY THINGS; DO ONE.

Portuguese Proverb

WEEKLY TRACKER

MY WEEKLY WINS

_____

_____

_____

THIS WEEK, I LEARNT

_____

_____

_____

HABIT TRACKER

HABIT	M	T	W	T	F	S	S
	●	●	●	●	●	●	●
	●	●	●	●	●	●	●
	●	●	●	●	●	●	●

MY TASKS FOR NEXT WEEK

- ◯
- ◯
- ◯
- ◯
- ◯
- ◯
- ◯

DATE _____   M T W T F S S

MY INTENTION FOR THE DAY IS

_____

_____

THIS IS HOW I WILL MAKE TODAY GREAT

_____

TOP THREE TASKS   ## DAILY SCHEDULE

- O _____ | TIME | TASK |
- O _____ | --- | --- |
- O _____ | | |
                             | | |
OTHER TASKS | | |
                             | | |
- O _____ | | |
- O _____ | | |
- O _____ | | |
- O _____ | | |
- O _____ | | |
- O _____ | | |
- O _____ | | |
- O _____ | | |
- O _____ | | |
- O _____ | | |
- O _____ | | |
- O _____ | | |
- O _____ | | |

DAILY TRACKER

LAST NIGHT, I DREAMT

MY BEST THOUGHTS WERE

MY REWARD FOR MEETING MY GOALS IS

TODAY, I FEEL

EXCELLENT   GOOD   REGULAR   SAD   ANGRY

DAILY TRACKER

SLEEP

DATE _____   (M T W T F S S

MY INTENTION FOR THE DAY IS

_____

_____

THIS IS HOW I WILL MAKE TODAY GREAT

_____

_____

TOP THREE TASKS

- ○ _____
- ○ _____
- ○ _____

OTHER TASKS

- ○ _____
- ○ _____
- ○ _____
- ○ _____
- ○ _____
- ○ _____
- ○ _____
- ○ _____
- ○ _____
- ○ _____
- ○ _____
- ○ _____
- ○ _____

DAILY SCHEDULE

TIME	TASK

DAILY TRACKER

LAST NIGHT, I DREAMT

MY BEST THOUGHTS WERE

MY REWARD FOR MEETING MY GOALS IS

TODAY, I FEEL

EXCELLENT   GOOD   REGULAR   SAD   ANGRY

DAILY TRACKER

SLEEP

DATE _____

MY INTENTION FOR THE DAY IS

_____

_____

THIS IS HOW I WILL MAKE TODAY GREAT

_____

_____

TOP THREE TASKS

O _____

O _____

O _____

OTHER TASKS

O _____

O _____

O _____

O _____

O _____

O _____

O _____

O _____

O _____

O _____

O _____

O _____

O _____

DAILY SCHEDULE

TIME	TASK

DAILY TRACKER

LAST NIGHT, I DREAMT

_____

_____

_____

MY BEST THOUGHTS WERE

_____

_____

_____

MY REWARD FOR MEETING MY GOALS IS

_____

_____

_____

TODAY, I FEEL

EXCELLENT   GOOD   REGULAR   SAD   ANGRY

DAILY TRACKER

SLEEP

DATE _____

MY INTENTION FOR THE DAY IS

_____

_____

THIS IS HOW I WILL MAKE TODAY GREAT

_____

_____

TOP THREE TASKS

O _____

O _____

O _____

OTHER TASKS

O _____
O _____
O _____
O _____
O _____
O _____
O _____
O _____
O _____
O _____
O _____
O _____
O _____

DAILY SCHEDULE

TIME	TASK

DAILY TRACKER

LAST NIGHT, I DREAMT

MY BEST THOUGHTS WERE

MY REWARD FOR MEETING MY GOALS IS

TODAY, I FEEL

EXCELLENT

GOOD

REGULAR

SAD

ANGRY

DAILY TRACKER

SLEEP

DATE _____   M T W T F S

MY INTENTION FOR THE DAY IS

_____

_____

THIS IS HOW I WILL MAKE TODAY GREAT

_____

TOP THREE TASKS

○ _____
○ _____
○ _____

OTHER TASKS

○ _____
○ _____
○ _____
○ _____
○ _____
○ _____
○ _____
○ _____
○ _____
○ _____
○ _____
○ _____
○ _____

DAILY SCHEDULE

TIME	TASK

DAILY TRACKER

LAST NIGHT, I DREAMT

MY BEST THOUGHTS WERE

MY REWARD FOR MEETING MY GOALS IS

TODAY, I FEEL

EXCELLENT

GOOD

REGULAR

SAD

ANGRY

DAILY TRACKER

SLEEP

DATE _____   M T W T F S

MY INTENTION FOR THE DAY IS

_____

_____

THIS IS HOW I WILL MAKE TODAY GREAT

_____

TOP THREE TASKS

- ○ _____
- ○ _____
- ○ _____

OTHER TASKS

- ○ _____
- ○ _____
- ○ _____
- ○ _____
- ○ _____
- ○ _____
- ○ _____
- ○ _____
- ○ _____
- ○ _____
- ○ _____
- ○ _____
- ○ _____

DAILY SCHEDULE

TIME	TASK

DAILY TRACKER

LAST NIGHT, I DREAMT

MY BEST THOUGHTS WERE

MY REWARD FOR MEETING MY GOALS IS

TODAY, I FEEL

EXCELLENT

GOOD

REGULAR

SAD

ANGRY

DAILY TRACKER

SLEEP

DATE _____   (M T W T F S

MY INTENTION FOR THE DAY IS

_____

_____

THIS IS HOW I WILL MAKE TODAY GREAT

_____

_____

TOP THREE TASKS

- O _____
- O _____
- O _____

OTHER TASKS

- O _____
- O _____
- O _____
- O _____
- O _____
- O _____
- O _____
- O _____
- O _____
- O _____
- O _____
- O _____
- O _____

DAILY SCHEDULE

TIME	TASK

DAILY TRACKER

LAST NIGHT, I DREAMT

MY BEST THOUGHTS WERE

MY REWARD FOR MEETING MY GOALS IS

TODAY, I FEEL

| EXCELLENT | GOOD | REGULAR | SAD | ANGRY |

DAILY TRACKER

SLEEP

THE VERY LEAST YOU
CAN DO IN YOUR LIFE
IS FIGURE OUT WHAT
YOU HOPE FOR.
AND THE MOST YOU
CAN DO IS LIVE
INSIDE THAT HOPE.

Barbara Kingsolver

bonus days.

TAKE A MOMENT

DATE _____

MY INTENTION FOR THE DAY IS

_____

_____

THIS IS HOW I WILL MAKE TODAY GREAT

_____

TOP THREE TASKS

○ _____
○ _____
○ _____

OTHER TASKS

○ _____
○ _____
○ _____
○ _____
○ _____
○ _____
○ _____
○ _____
○ _____
○ _____
○ _____
○ _____
○ _____

DAILY SCHEDULE

TIME	TASK

DAILY TRACKER

LAST NIGHT, I DREAMT

MY BEST THOUGHTS WERE

MY REWARD FOR MEETING MY GOALS IS

TODAY, I FEEL

EXCELLENT   GOOD   REGULAR   SAD   ANGRY

DAILY TRACKER

SLEEP

DATE _____

MY INTENTION FOR THE DAY IS

_____

_____

THIS IS HOW I WILL MAKE TODAY GREAT

_____

TOP THREE TASKS

○ _____

○ _____

○ _____

OTHER TASKS

○ _____
○ _____
○ _____
○ _____
○ _____
○ _____
○ _____
○ _____
○ _____
○ _____
○ _____
○ _____
○ _____

DAILY SCHEDULE

TIME	TASK

DAILY TRACKER

LAST NIGHT, I DREAMT

MY BEST THOUGHTS WERE

MY REWARD FOR MEETING MY GOALS IS

TODAY, I FEEL

EXCELLENT

GOOD

REGULAR

SAD

ANGRY

DAILY TRACKER

SLEEP

DATE _____

M T W T F S S

MY INTENTION FOR THE DAY IS

_____

_____

THIS IS HOW I WILL MAKE TODAY GREAT

_____

TOP THREE TASKS

○ _____

○ _____

○ _____

OTHER TASKS

○ _____
○ _____
○ _____
○ _____
○ _____
○ _____
○ _____
○ _____
○ _____
○ _____
○ _____
○ _____
○ _____

DAILY SCHEDULE

TIME	TASK

DAILY TRACKER

LAST NIGHT, I DREAMT

MY BEST THOUGHTS WERE

MY REWARD FOR MEETING MY GOALS IS

TODAY, I FEEL

EXCELLENT

GOOD

REGULAR

SAD

ANGRY

DAILY TRACKER

SLEEP

THERE IS ALWAYS LIGHT,
IF ONLY WE'RE BRAVE
ENOUGH TO SEE IT.
IF ONLY WE'RE BRAVE
ENOUGH TO BE IT.

Amanda Gorman

WEEKLY TRACKER

THIS WEEK, I LEARNT

HABIT TRACKER

HABIT	M	T	W	T	F	S	S
	●	●	●	●	●	●	●
	●	●	●	●	●	●	●
	●	●	●	●	●	●	●

MY TASKS FOR NEXT WEEK

common dreams.

AND WHAT THEY MEAN

Every night, you can expect to have around three to six dream cycles, each one typically lasting for between 5 and 20 minutes. Researchers are still scratching their heads at the role of this nightly occurrence, with theories ranging from psychotherapy to the processing of daily information. Although dream experiences vary widely between one person and another, nearly everybody has them; some people even dream about the same subject repeatedly. In fact, there are ten types of dreams that are experienced—at least once—by most people across all cultures. Making a record of these dreams in particular could help you understand the emotions that may be behind them.

THE DREAM WHERE YOUR TEETH ARE FALLING OUT

WHAT DO THE EXPERTS THINK?
This is often connected with anxieties about how others perceive you. It could also tie in with any communication difficulties you may have when trying to express yourself.

WHAT DO YOU THINK?

THE DREAM WHERE YOU ARE BEING CHASED

WHAT DO THE EXPERTS THINK?

You might be avoiding an issue or a person. Pay special attention to who or what is chasing you. If it's someone you know, for example; what kind of person are they? If they're judgemental, the dream could reflect your own overcritical voice. If you're being chased by an animal, think about what that animal means to you. A fierce lion might signify that you lack the courage to face difficulties.

WHAT DO YOU THINK?

THE DREAM WHERE YOU ARE NAKED

WHAT DO THE EXPERTS THINK?

This dream could indicate anxiety about threats to your own safety and well-being. You may feel exposed, vulnerable or insecure.

WHAT DO YOU THINK?

THE DREAM WHERE YOU CAN'T FIND A TOILET

WHAT DO THE EXPERTS THINK?

Searching for a toilet might just mean that you need to wake up and relieve yourself. However, if you can't find the toilet in the dream, it may be related to a specific need or desire you're not having met.

WHAT DO YOU THINK?

_____

_____

_____

_____

THE DREAM WHERE YOU ARE UNPREPARED FOR AN EXAM

WHAT DO THE EXPERTS THINK?

At least one in five people dream about their fears when facing an exam or test. These dreams typically reflect on the person's lack of confidence or inability to move to the next stage in their life.

WHAT DO YOU THINK?

_____

_____

_____

_____

THE DREAM WHERE YOU ARE FLYING

WHAT DO THE EXPERTS THINK?

Flying dreams tend to be associated with a sense of freedom and momentum. Do you feel restricted in any way? Or on the other hand, have you found a new sense of freedom recently? Either of these experiences could be related to this dream.

WHAT DO YOU THINK?

THE DREAM WHERE WHERE YOU ARE FALLING

WHAT DO THE EXPERTS THINK?

You may be struggling with fear or anxiety about failing after recently failing at something or fearing that you will.

WHAT DO YOU THINK?

THE DREAM WHERE YOU FIND AN NEW ROOM

WHAT DO THE EXPERTS THINK?

Discovering a new room in your dream may be related to a new outlook or ability you've recently uncovered within yourself.

WHAT DO YOU THINK?

THE DREAM INVOLVING INFIDELITY

WHAT DO THE EXPERTS THINK?

These dreams are often associated with real-life anxieties about relationships, and can result from underlying trust issues. Dreams where you are the cheater might mean you believe you're giving too much time and attention to someone or something else in your life. In other instances, these dreams can relate to a difficult decision you need to make or to general turmoil within your life.

WHAT DO YOU THINK?

notes and ideas.

LEARN FROM YESTERDAY

NOTES & IDEAS

NOTES & IDEAS

NOTES & IDEAS

NOTES & IDEAS

NOTES & IDEAS

NOTES & IDEAS

NOTES & IDEAS

NOTES & IDEAS

NOTES & IDEAS

NOTES & IDEAS

NOTES & IDEAS

NOTES & IDEAS

REFERENCES

Page 5. Boldness has genius in it.
Johann Wolfgang von Goethe, (1835): Faust, Part 1

Page 28. We must not only act, but also dream.
Anatole France, (1896). An introductory speech at a session of the Académie Française

Page 44. Dreams are lovely. But they are just dreams.
Shonda Rhimes, (2015). Year of Yes: How to Dance It Out, Stand In the Sun and Be Your Own Person

Page 60. Effectiveness by doing.
Amelia Earhart: http://ameliaearhart.com/, The Family of Amelia Earhart

Page 76. Consistency shapes our lives.
Tony Robbins, (1991): Awaken the Giant Within: How to Take Immediate Control of Your Mental, Emotional, Physical and Financial Destiny!

Page 96. Paint your dream.
Vincent van Gogh (1853– 1890): https://www.recorder.com/Archives/2015/07/AE-072315-GR-Van-Gogh-Stewart

Page 112. Give all to the present.
Albert Camus, (1935-1942): Notebooks

Page 128. Make the days count.
Muhammad Ali: https://www.espn.com/box story/_/id/15930888/muhammad-ali-10-b quotes

Page 144. The key to great art.
Beyoncé Giselle Knowles-Carter, (2020), Be Vogue

Page 164. Start now.
Arthur Ashe: https://www.entrepreneur.c article/33854

Page 180. Make your world.
Toni Morrison, (1992): Jazz

Page 196. Think of many things; do one.
Portuguese Proverb: Diana Delonzor, (20 Never Be Late Again, 7 Cures for the Punct Challenged

Page 212. Figure out what you hope for.
Barbara Kingsolver, (1990): Animal Dreams

Page 228. There is always light.
Amanda Gorman, (2021): The Hill We Cli recited at the 2021 presidential inaugura ceremony